GAMES FOR ANIMAL LOVERS

GAMES TO MAKE YOU LAUGH

GAMES TO SCARE YOU

GAMES FOR BUILDERS

LOOKING FRESH

GAMES FOR PVP

GAMES FOR GOING FAST

GAMES FOR LEARNING

GAMES FOR BEGINNERS

GAMES FOR PRETENDING

GAMES FOR A CHALLENGE

Published 2023. Little Brother Books Ltd, Ground Floor, 23 Southernhay East, Exeter, Devon, EX1 1QL
Printed in China.
EU address: Korte Leemstraat 3, 2018 Antwerpen, Belgium
books@littlebrotherbooks.co.uk www.littlebrotherbooks.co.uk

WHAT IS ROBLOX?

Roblox has **amazing** games and **brilliant** events. There are plenty of places you and your friends can gather to **chat**, **play** and **hang out**. Imagination and adventure are waiting for you. Let's jump in, and find out more.

GAMES

The leading reason so many people use Roblox is the number of games that can be played. It doesn't matter who you are or what kind of games you like, you will find something here to enjoy. Roblox has hundreds of thousands of games to try and they are handily arranged for you to find something new, popular or ideal for you.

Discover

Most Engaging

| Easy Fun Obby | Mega Obby | Build to Survive! | Pop It Trading | Flee the Facility | Adopt a Baby! | Murder Mystery 2 | Maple Hospital [BLACKOUT!] |

Recommended For You

| Brookhaven RP | Adopt Me! | Berry Avenue RP | Tower of Hell | Murder Mystery 2 | Teamwork Puzzles 2 (Obby) | DOORS | Piggy |

Free Kitten   108 Sec

Buy Kitten! +3 Kittens Kittens

+20070

710K   1.97M

EXPRESSION

It's possible to use Roblox to express yourself. You can change how you look, creating a new 'online' version of you. It's not just about changing a shirt or a pair of shoes, if you want, you can become an animal, or an alien. The only limit, is your imagination, you can be as sensible, or as silly as you want.

STAYING CONNECTED

Roblox allows you to stay connected with friends and family easily. If you're missing your cousin or a friend who moved to a new area, you can join them for a game, wherever they are in the world. You can meet new friends while playing, and some lucky students even get to learn about science or history through Roblox, with their teacher and the rest of their class.

ROBLOX DOESN'T ONLY HOST LOTS OF PLAYERS, BUT ALSO LOTS OF EXPERIENCES. THERE ARE OVER 40 MILLION EXPERIENCES TO BE EXPLORED.

FREE HAT!

NIKELAND

49   278   ♪   BROL ⏸ ⏭

ME

QU
Talk to Nik

GEORGE EZRA

THE GOLD RUSH KID EXPERIENCE

Gold Rush Kid

George Ezra's Gold Rush Kid Experience
By Gold Rush Friends
All Ages

▶

Favorite   Follow   6,218   3,451

About   Store   Servers

Description

Welcome to George Ezra's Gold Rush Kid Experience! Take a trip through the world of award-winning English musician George Ezra's latest album, Gold Rush Kid. There's lots to do around the space:
- Fly thru the hoops in the Blue Blue Sky w/ a cool plane!
- Explore the village to find puzzle pieces & complete the jigsaw for an exclusive reward!
- Test your knowledge of George & the village in a 4-Choice Quiz!
- Stop by "The Gold Rush" shop for virtual merchandise

ROBLOX IS PLAYED ACROSS THE WORLD BY OVER 22 MILLION PLAYERS PER DAY. THAT'S TWICE AS MANY PEOPLE WHO LIVE IN BELGIUM!

EXPERIENCES

Did you know that Roblox often hosts great experiences with pop stars, sports and TV companies as well as joining up with the latest movies? One day you can be exploring behind the scenes of a blockbuster film, the next day you can dance at a concert with your friends.

YOUR ROBLOX

Your Roblox journey starts here. By **creating a profile**, you can venture out into a world of games and experiences. Your profile is your little corner of Roblox; a place to **show off what you love** about Roblox.

PROFILE PAGE

Your profile page contains information about you that other people can read. It gives them an idea about you, what you play and what you enjoy. You can write an introduction about yourself for other players to learn more about you. Why not write something to make them laugh, or talk about the things you love in life.

There's a space that shows the games you've selected as favourites, and another that

displays badges you've unlocked while playing. Badges are awards for unlocking things in games. These two sections show off your personality and the games you play a lot.

Another section shows your friends and those you've made while playing. You can accept or ignore friend requests here. Checking this page will show what your friends are playing right now. You can even jump into their game!

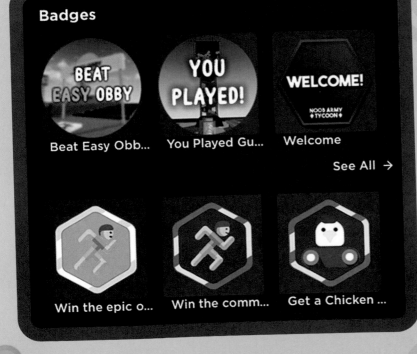

EVEN THOUGH THIS IS YOUR SPACE TO PERSONALISE, YOU MUST REMEMBER TO STAY SAFE WHEN CREATING YOUR INTRODUCTION: DON'T INCLUDE ANY PERSONAL INFORMATION. SOMETIMES IT HELPS TO CREATE THIS WITH A PARENT NEARBY WHO CAN READ IT THROUGH.

JOURNEY

When **creating your avatar**, you can choose to be as wacky or serious as you'd like. There are hundreds of options to choose from and plenty more you can buy using 'real money'. Remember that **your avatar is what everyone will see** in games.

AVATAR CREATION

ITEMS IN THE AVATAR SHOP COST ROBUX TO BUY, AND ROBUX IS BOUGHT WITH REAL MONEY. YOU CAN BUY ROBUX THROUGH YOUR DIGITAL WALLET, OR AS GIFT CARDS IN SHOPS AND SUPERMARKETS. REMEMBER, YOU WILL NEED A PARENT'S PERMISSION BEFORE MAKING ANY PAYMENTS.

STEP-BY-STEP
Start off by choosing a body type and face that you like. You can build your avatar from here. You can expand this by choosing things like height, as well as hairstyle. Next comes clothing and accessories like glasses, hats and bags.

If you take a trip over to the Marketplace, you'll discover a huge collection of items that can be used to make your avatar look even more spectacular. There are thousands of items to be bought - if you can think of it, someone has probably created it

and listed it for sale. There are lots of items available for free and many games and experiences offer items to unlock for completing tasks.

Once you've chosen everything you want to equip, check out how your avatar looks in 2D and 3D - just in

case something doesn't look as cool as you thought it would. You can change your avatar as often as you like, so visit regularly.

USING THE SEARCH FUNCTION, YOU CAN SEARCH FOR ANY TOPIC YOU WANT. GIVE IT A TRY - SEARCH FOR 'BUNNY EARS', OR 'WIZARD HAT'. WHAT ABOUT 'DINOSAUR CLAWS'?

ACCOUNT SETTINGS

Making sure you have the **right settings** turned on will allow you to play the **right games** for your age range. You can also give Roblox information to make your experience better.

My Settings

Account Info
Security
Privacy
Billing
Notifications

Account Info

Display Name: Display Name

Username: Username

Password: ******

Phone Number:

Email Address:

Personal

Birthday — Month / Day / Year

ⓘ Updating age to under 13 will enable Privacy Mode.

Verify My Age

By clicking 'Verify My Age' you will be completing an ID verification process operated by our third party service provider.

Gender (Optional)

Language — Language

Location — Country

Theme — Dark

ACCOUNT INFO

This page allows you to set a username for your account. This is a name that will be displayed to other players and what they use to add you as a friend or invite you to a game. You'll also see an area for your birthday. Details input here can verify your age and identity to keep you safer.

SECURITY AND PRIVACY

This section of the account sets who can contact you, who can see when you're playing and if they can add you to their friends list. These are important options; if your contact details are open to everyone, then anyone in the world can send you a message.

My Settings

Account Info
Security
Privacy
Billing
Parental Controls
App Permissions

What are Parental Controls?

Parental Controls allow parents to choose the correct settings that will control what experiences their child can access.

Parent PIN

Parent PIN is disabled

When this setting is enabled, the PIN must be provided before changing settings.

Allowed Experiences

All experiences are searchable. Experiences without Experience Guidelines are treated as 13+ and are prohibited from displaying any 17+ content. All content on Roblox must comply with the Roblox Community Standards.

● 13+ (Suitable for ages 13 and older)

○ 9+ (Suitable for ages 9 and older)

○ All Ages (Suitable for everyone)

PARENTAL

This important section controls what games and experiences you can join in with. Your parent will find some options for your age group and depending on which option is selected this will determine which experiences are available to you. If you have 9+ (suitable for ages 9 and older) selected, you won't be able to play games designed for players older than 9 years old.

ROBUX

Robux is a **digital currency** that can only be spent in Roblox. Anything you want to buy on the Roblox platform, including items in the **Avatar Shop** or **private servers**, will cost a set amount of Robux.

Robux can be purchased in several ways; as gift cards from your local supermarket or directly in-game. You can also sign up for Roblox Premium, which delivers a number of Robux to your account each month.

If you choose to buy Robux in-game, you will need to assign a payment card. This can be a parent's card, meaning you'll need permission to buy Robux beforehand.

Buy Robux

Robux allows you to purchase upgrades for your avatar or buy special abilities in experiences.

	Robux Packages ⓘ	Subscribe and Get More ⓘ
£4.99	◎ 400	◎ 450/month
£9.99	◎ 800	◎ 1,000/month
£19.99	◎ 1,700	◎ 2,200/month
£49.99	◎ 4,500	Not Available
£99.99	◎ 10,000	Not Available

ALWAYS BE AWARE OF ROBUX SCAMS. IF ANYONE IN A GAME IS OFFERING FREE ROBUX, IT'S LIKELY THAT THEY CANNOT BE TRUSTED.

Category
- All Items
- Characters
- Clothing
- Accessories
- Heads
- Animations

Filters

Sales Type
- All
- Limited
- Premium

Creator
- All Creators

Go

Price
- Any Price

Go

Sorts
- Relevance
- Most Favorited
- Bestselling
- Recently Created
- Price (High to Low)
- Price (Low to High)

All Items

monkey   piercing   scary   scrunchie   frog   half   watermelon   banana   disgusted   fursuit   visor   earring   cross

Joyful Smile ◎ 20
Robloxian 2.0 ◎ 15
Err... ◎ 70
:] ◎ 15
Melon Head ◎ 20
Cheeks ◎ 75

Firey Pom Poms of Eternal ◎ 9
Dizzy Face ◎ 30
Black to White Fluffy Messy Cool By @PointMelon ◎ 55
Bored ◎ 25

Overseer Oversleeper: ◎ 100
YAAAWWN. ◎ 50
TanqR Mask By @TanqR ◎ 50
Black Straigh... ◎ 25

THERE ARE PLENTY OF FREE ITEMS FOR YOUR AVATAR AND REMEMBER THESE ITEMS DON'T CHANGE ANYTHING ABOUT THE GAME, BESIDES CHANGING THE LOOK OF YOUR AVATAR.

Many items you'll see for sale can be very cheap - under 100 Robux. However, you'll also see some super expensive items too. Thankfully you won't be able to accidentally buy anything if you don't have the Robux in your account!

If you are a creative person, you could always use Roblox Studio to create your own items which can be sold for Robux. This can then be spent within the game, or converted to 'real world money'.

With so many games that allow you to become an animal or collect lots of different pets, animal lovers have plenty to choose from. Explore these games and see if you can find your favourite animal here.

PET SIMULATOR X!

One of the most popular **pet games** isn't just about pets. *Pet Simulator X!* combines two types of game - **pet adoption** and **mining for materials**.

In this bright and colourful world, it's your job to become as powerful as you can through mining piles of coins. The way to do this, is to adopt strong pets who can break open anything.

There are several areas to explore - Shop, Town, Forest, there's a Beach and a Cave too. Not long after you've made your way through these starter areas, you'll find new worlds to explore, often themed around a holiday like Easter or Christmas. Scattered throughout these worlds are piles of gold and each time you break them open, you're showered in coins and gems.

Players can spend coins on eggs in the shop to hatch new pets. These pets can be combined or turned into golden, or rainbow versions which make them more powerful. More power means breaking open bigger piles of gold, or chests, or even bank vaults! All the time, your pets will be working away mining objects.

As you travel through each world they get more and more bonkers, taking you under the ocean, or into Heaven. The more you play, the more coins you'll collect and slowly you'll complete tasks which boost your rank - the highest rank being 'THE BEST'. Who doesn't want to be the best at a game?

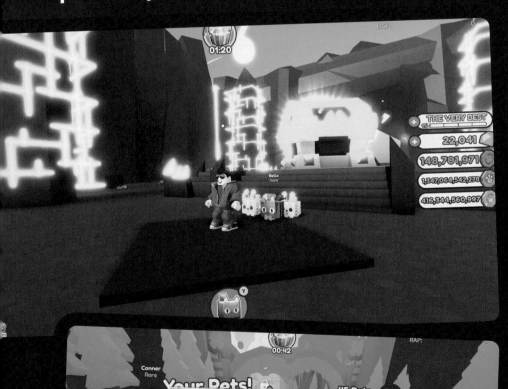

BAD CAT

You've all seen those videos on YouTube, it's a compilation showing **clips of cats** knocking glasses off tables or dangling from the curtains. This is **your chance** to be one of those cats.

Everything starts off quite small; you're a cat who has one job and that is to destroy the apartment you've been left in. You claw and scratch at the sofa, at the TV. Even the fridge falls to pieces as you continue to whack it. You're surrounded by other cats, with players sat at home controlling the chaos.

Soon, the apartment is too small for you and the world outside is calling. From here you'll leave a trail of destruction through playgrounds, office buildings and the natural world. Trees fall down, washing machines explode and lamps shatter to the ground. All the while your owner is commenting what a bad kitty you are.

In only a short amount of time you'll be hitting cars, watching as the wheels fall off and the engine explodes in a fireball. Naughty kitty cat! The main thing to achieve is a high score through destroying as much as you can and levelling up your cat to access new areas.

To top it all off, quite literally, you can equip your cat with funny little hats. These can be collected through playing, or bought with Robux. Then your fluffy ball of destruction will just look like a goofy little guy.

BEE TYCOON

Bee Tycoon, like so many other tycoon games, asks you to make **as much money** as possible. It's pretty simple, all players need to do is wait for bees to **make honey.**

Honey appears as small colourful balls to be collected. This is then deposited into a machine which jars and sells the honey.

In order to upgrade your honey farm, you'll need to save money and walk over buttons to action the upgrade. The wonderful thing about *Bee Tycoon* is the merging of bees. At first you'll just have bees in yellow honeycomb shapes. However, if you merge these together they create brown bees. Merging brown bees makes green, green make blue and so on.

The different colours produce more valuable honey. For example, a ball of blue honey will be worth a lot more than yellow honey. This money can improve your honey station, or buy a lot more bees! If you want to earn even more money, there's an obby to play. Once you complete the obby, you're rewarded with 2x the honey.

This is a great tycoon for those who aren't sure where to begin with tycoon games. It's very simple compared to others, starting you off slow and steady.

IF YOU LIKE THIS, YOU'LL LOVE MEGA MANSION TYCOON.

PET SWARM SIMULATOR

Pet Swarm Simulator is a role-playing game where players **hatch** and **care** for **cool pets** who are then used to harvest materials or fight monsters.

The land of Pet Swarmia has been cursed by an evil Wizard, turning lots of cute animals into scary monsters. It's up to you to fight back against this evil.

In your home nest you can place eggs which will hatch into creatures. They might be cute looking dogs or more monstrous fantasy animals. As you explore the world around you, you'll notice fruits that you can harvest which can be used to help hatch more eggs and also collect gold coins.

For a boost in earnings, you can approach local farmers and work with them on the quests they hand out. They might want you to rid the area of evil creatures, rewarding you with more coins that you can spend opening new areas with more interesting pets.

You'll need to be careful though, your pets can be injured while fighting monsters! If you try to fight a monster too soon, you could end up back at your nest after your pets are knocked out.

ADOPT ME!

Adopt Me! is the most **popular** game on Roblox, having **millions** of visitors per day. It's easy to see why it's so popular - **collecting** and **trading** pets is so much fun! There are hundreds of pets to collect, and new animals are released **every** few weeks, or around seasonal events such as Christmas, Easter and Halloween. There's never been a better time to **start adopting**.

Adopt Me! **can feel a little overwhelming as you first enter Adoption Island. There are lots of shops and businesses scattered around to explore, but the most important place to visit is the nursery. It's here that you will be buying eggs that will hatch into different animals.**

In order to buy eggs, you need to earn money by interacting with your first pet that is given to you for free. By cleaning them, feeding them and making sure they get enough sleep, you will be rewarded with cash. This is what you need to buy food and drink, but also get new eggs and start building your pet collection.

There are around 200 pets in *Adopt Me!* at the moment and they come in all shapes and sizes - from small dogs to large dragons. These pets can be traded with other players or, if you have lots of copies of animals, you can combine them to create neon versions of the pet which changes their colour.

Don't worry, it doesn't stop there. Those neon pets? They can also be combined together to create MEGA NEON animals, which make them the rarest animals.

TIPS AND TRICKS

COMPLETE TASKS GIVEN BY YOUR PET

Your pet will often ask you to perform certain tasks; things like going to certain shops, feeding them, or playing with them. These tasks reward you with cash.

DON'T WASTE YOUR MONEY

It's so easy to get caught up in buying lots of items and accessories, but if your goal is to collect as many pets as possible, you'll need the money for eggs. Try to spend your cash on eggs first, then when you have your pets, spend elsewhere.

LOG-IN STREAKS

Adopt Me! offers log-in streaks, which means you must be in the game every day. You don't have to play, you can just log-in, claim the reward, then close the game. The higher your streak, the better rewards you can claim when you play.

BEWARE OF TRADING

Try to stick to trading with friends whenever you can. You will be able to trust them, plus you can all work together to hatch the correct pets for neon creation.

STICK WITH YOUR JOB

Your job in *Adopt Me!* will give you regular payments as long as you complete tasks and it's a quick way to get rich. Make sure you collect the payments when they pop up on screen.

Laughter can come from anything. Maybe it's a silly amount of destruction, or monsters stomping around chasing after your mates. Laughter is is good for you and these games might just brighten your day.

RAT WASHING TYCOON

There aren't many games sillier than *Rat Washing Tycoon*. **Who pays to have their rats washed?** Who even sets up a business washing rats? Why are the rats all funny shapes?

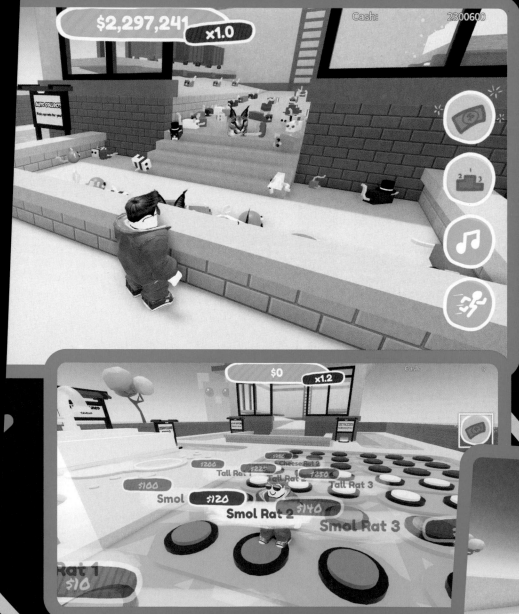

You won't get any answers to those questions here, but you will have a few laughs while collecting hundreds of rats and giving them a good scrub. You start off with nice normal rats. These are the kinds you'd find in a pet shop. You collect them from the central building and dump them into your sink.

Now you can start earning money! Washing the rats will earn you cash that can be spent on upgrading your sink station, or unlocking new rats. It's the new rats players will love. Long rats; sphere rats; rats that look like bees; rats with posh top hats; donut rats. There's even a rat eating soup from a bowl.

Each of these funky new rats will earn you more cash, and you'll need it. While the early rats are quite cheap, the weirder ones start to cost hundreds of thousands of dollars. Thankfully there's a very easy obby which rewards you with 2x income for a minute. Drag your friends in and see who can wash the most rats... that was a strange sentence.

BROKEN BONES IV

On-screen game HUD elements:

STOP

0
0
0
0

457 Meters
37 Mph

RS

$ 1,676,693

Level 18

[Shift Key]
Helium Balloon

LS

Level	Name
33	Jaydennnnn36
31	cookiefr01
19	iitox1cv1bes
18	Amisma48
15	florentin59123
14	gorster20105
13	Andrewwalker57890
11	MRLover1020
10	Davidgabor22725
8	navyavengers
6	davud12345pr
5	hwhwuqij
4	SnowDoge25

Do not attempt to recreate any of the stunts from this game. **Seriously**, if you broke this many bones at once, you'd be all **floppy**, like a **jelly** person.

The name of this game kind of gives away what you'll be doing. The goal is to break your avatar's bones and ligaments. Basically break as much as possible to score cash payouts. The more bones you break, the more cash you get.

At the start of each round, players need to jump off tall cliffs and slam, skid or bounce their way across the ground. You can use power ups which catapult you into the air, or blast you into the sides of mountains. This ends when your avatar's body comes to a stop at the bottom, where you're shown a rewards screen of an x-ray with plenty of broken bones.

As you play, you can upgrade abilities to help you score more points. Putting money into bouncing allows you to spring up from the ground and slam back down; while air time makes you stay in the air longer, for a bigger landing.

It's hilarious watching all these avatars flying through the air, landing with a crunch. Your arms and legs will be waggling all over the place while you spin and somersault with no grace at all. Don't gets us started on the crunchy, crackly sound effects!

TORNADO SIMULATOR

Destruction – **pretend destruction**, at least - can be great fun. **Smashing** things, **breaking** furniture and causing a mess. It'll get you into trouble in life, but not on Roblox.

There are many things you can become across Roblox. Usually it's animals or other people, but here you get to be a tornado. The gameplay is familiar - you'll be collecting items and selling them in order to upgrade. Except here, you're tearing the items from the ground.

As you whirl and swirl around the map, you'll be pulling street furniture into your gusty guts. The objects you pass over will end up spinning around your tornado slowly adding to the size of your tornado. As you grow larger, you'll be collecting larger items. Starting with rubbish bags, moving on to trees and cars.

The upgrades will allow bigger tornados, faster movement and more money from items you sell. It doesn't take long before you're spinning across the city yanking up buildings. You can't help but smile as your tiny tornado rapidly grows and you're clearing the entire map of houses, vehicles and skyscrapers.

It's great to watch other people play too, especially the experienced players who grow so big that they eclipse the sky!

SHARKBITE 2

Will **you** become the predator? Or perhaps try to survive one of the world's **most ferocious animals** as it rampages through the ocean?

Sharkbite 2 **is a great game, but it becomes a lot better with a bunch of friends. This is due to how it plays. When the game starts, your group will be split up with one person becoming the shark. It's their job to cruise through the water looking to chomp up boats and people.**

The rest of the group will become survivors. All they need to do is avoid the shark for as long as possible, or even eliminate it using a selection of weapons.

If you're all talking to each other in voice chat, the laughs will start pretty quickly. As soon as the shark bursts from the water, it's hard to know whether to shoot or try to get away. Nothing beats playing as the shark and gobbling up your friends as they squeal and giggle.

Or, you can group together as survivors and try to take out the shark. Some of you are bound to get eaten, but that's the price to pay for a fun game of chase.

BOOK OF MONSTERS

Book of Monsters is complete **chaos**. It's a whirlwind of **destruction**, with monsters trying to destroy **everything** they see and players attempting to take down the monsters in any way they can.

If you've ever seen a monster movie, this game might be familiar to you. As you drop into the game, the first thing you'll see is a group of wacky monsters stomping around the area. They will cause no end of carnage as they break buildings into pieces. This mayhem can only be stopped by the survivors.

But how can you stop them? Each of these monsters has a big red button on their back. If someone ever told you not to press any big red buttons, they were wrong. Jumping onto this button will hurt the monster, removing one of their hearts. You must remove all hearts to beat them and win the round.

All survivors are equipped with a tool, like a trampoline to bounce up and reach the button; a weapon to break cages that at times will cover the button; and a roll to dodge out of the way. You will definitely need this roll, because the monsters hit hard!

You only have three hearts which will break one at a time if a monster manages to stomp on you. Lose all three and you'll be sent back to the lobby.

Perhaps the best part of *Book of Monsters* is the monsters themselves.

> PLAYING ON YOUR OWN AS A SURVIVOR CAN BE TRICKY - IT'S EASY TO GET STOMPED ON. IF YOU PLAY AS A TEAM WITH FRIENDS, YOU CAN SWARM THE MONSTERS AND KEEP THEM DISTRACTED WHILE YOU ALL GO FOR THE BUTTON.

Juggernaut 3:55

THERE ARE LOTS OF MAPS TO CHOOSE FROM IN *BOOK OF MONSTERS*, AND WHILE THEY ALL LOOK GREAT, THE MAP YOU PLAY DOESN'T MATTER TOO MUCH. THIS IS BECAUSE WITHIN A MINUTE OR SO, THEY WILL ALL BE REDUCED TO RUBBLE ANYWAY.

They're wacky. You will fight anything from random animals to living toasters with a slice of bread poking out.

Of course, you might end up being selected to play as the monster. This completely changes how you will play the game and can be a lot more fun. Playing as a survivor is stressful - if you're unlucky you can get eliminated quickly. As the monster you get to smash buildings, launch players across the map with your attacks and generally be a nuisance.

It's your chance to live out all those action monster movies. Can you beat all the survivors and finally see the monsters win the war?

IF YOU'RE PLAYING AS THE MONSTER, NEVER STAND STILL. YOU HAVE TO KEEP MOVING. TRY SPINNING IN A CIRCLE IF YOU GET SURROUNDED TO KEEP THE SURVIVORS FROM REACHING YOUR BACK.

WHAT'S HAPPENING IN ROBLOX

Roblox is a **busy place** to be. It's not just games that you can experience, but also worlds **dedicated** to cartoons, or sports brands, there are also music concerts and **celebrations** of brand new films. The past year has seen **a lot** of excitement in Roblox!

GETTING MUSICAL

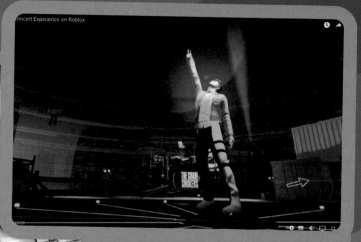

There have been plenty of music stars to recently pass through Roblox and put on 'out of this world' experiences. Bands like Chainsmokers entertained thousands of fans; Saweetie rolled through to celebrate the Super Bowl by performing in Rhythm City; and K-Pop legends NCT 127 launched their own experience for fans to explore.

ROBLOX WEEK

In July, creators from all over the world gathered together to celebrate Roblox. Over 1,500 Robloxians came together to talk about games, experiences and why we all love the game. It wasn't just creators, but also key people who work for Roblox - including Dave Baszucki who created Roblox back in 2006.

ANIME

The past year saw a huge leap in the number of games based on anime. As anime rises in popularity more and more people want to explore worlds inspired by the latest hits. We already had games like Box Fruits and Dragon Blox, now there are newer titles which bring all the worlds together, allowing you to play as your favourite characters. Check out All Star Tower Defence and Anime Adventures!

GROWING UP

Roblox has been available for a very long time now, and the creators who joined near the beginning are much older now. Roblox has had to grow alongside them, offering more and more ways to program new games. We're starting to see graphics that we never would have expected from Roblox a few years ago, and these games are getting larger in scale, too.

ROBLOX PETS

There are so many games that feature pets. A few years ago pets were only found in simulators or games like **Adopt Me!** Over time, **more** and **more** creators began adding pets to games of all kinds, usually starting out as eggs.

Collecting pets adds a whole new aspect to any game. Lots of games feature eggs that can be bought with in-game money that instantly hatch into cute pets, ranging from tiny dogs to large multicoloured dragons.

Many of these pets will be themed around worlds or areas in the game, and can also appear as part of an event for things like Easter, or Christmas. However, pets aren't there to just look cute, they often add a bonus to your character; for example, in *Mining Simulator*, the pets can speed up mining progress; or in *Laundry Simulator* they will pick up dirty clothes and place them in washing machines.

LET'S TAKE A LOOK AT A FEW GAMES THAT FEATURE LOTS OF FUN PETS.

SNOWBALLER SIMULATOR

This simulator game sees players trying to roll up the biggest snowball possible to let loose on a hill. As the snowball speeds along, it crashes into obstacles earning you points. Pets can wander alongside your avatar to speed up the rolling process and make better snowballs.

ROPETS

RoPets is a similar game to Adopt Me! You'll find yourself in a town, surrounded by other players whose goal is to collect as many pets as possible. RoPets looks very different though, it has a unique style and offers plenty of pets for new players.

RACE CLICKER

While you'll be clicking or tapping to build up speed in this racer, some pets will help build up that reserve of speed. Once the countdown ends, you'll dash along a lane of coloured tiles to see how far you can reach. The better the pets, the more speed, the better the outcome!

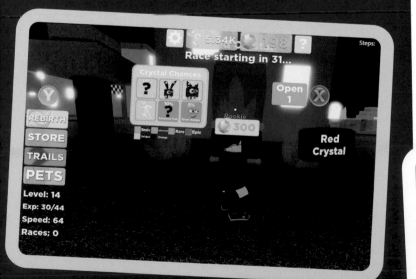

LEGENDS OF SPEED

The name of the game is what you're attempting to become - a legend of speed. Pets in this game help increase your average speed. This helps you win races and access different areas of the game world, to score more points and become a legend.

Being scared is an odd feeling. It's strangely something we enjoy, even though it should be something we avoid. Roblox is home to plenty of scary, spooky and frightening games that will test your nerves.

+500 EXP, +27c: *Headshot Kill*
+50 EXP, +4c: *Kill*

2630

20 4
180
AK-74u

MICHAEL'S ZOMBIES

At first look, *Michael's Zombies* feels a lot like *Call of Duty: World at War - Zombies* - there are **weapons**, **tools**, and of course, plenty of **undead**.

8
M1911 Colt

Press and hold X to repair barrier

3
M1911 Colt

Your task is to stay alive and leave the playing area via an escape route, this is usually in a vehicle of some sort. You can do this by eliminating zombies, which scores you points. These points are then spent on better weapons, traps and items which can heal you, or even revive you if you die.

There's an option to play by yourself on one of several maps, but the game becomes much harder without others. You need people to watch your back and thin the crowd of Zeds. It's really easy to get pinned in a corner and have your brain gobbled.

Once you've learned the maps and where the zombies spawn, you can quickly focus on staying alive. There are options to leave each map once you've survived long enough, which is considered 'winning the game' but if you're enjoying the scary atmosphere then stick around for longer and see how many zombies you can eliminate.

RAINBOW FRIENDS

The *Rainbow Friends* **want to play**. Unfortunately, on this school trip things aren't going well. Those 'Friends' seem to be **dangerous** and they're hunting **you** and your friends.

It's worth getting to know the various *Rainbow Friends* – Blue, Green, Orange and Purple. Blue is perhaps the easiest to recognise as their face is the first to appear, but the others want to get to know you. To make you their friend.

As with many other horror games on Roblox, the goal is to stay alive, hopefully finding items to save your friends along the way. Each round starts with players needing to locate particular items whilst avoiding the monsters. At the end of the round,

which takes place at night, survivors will go to a safe room before trying again.

Rainbow Friends is made scarier because of how friendly the monsters are supposed to be. Their bizarre smiles and bright eyes become very creepy when they're hunting for you along the corridors.

Learning how each monster moves and attacks is very important for survival. If you can stay alive, you can score that win and move onto the next chapter.

BLUE WILL SEARCH THE MAP FOR YOU. GREEN CAN'T SEE, SO WANDERS RANDOMLY. ORANGE FOLLOWS AN ORANGE LINE AND IS SUPER FAST. PURPLE ROAMS THROUGH THE AIR VENTS AND LURKS IN WATER.

PIGGY

Can you stay alive while being **hunted** by this family of pigs and their friends? Can you **escape** the map and live to see another day? Will you **uncover** the **secrets** hidden away in this survival horror?

08:59

08:23

This is where the signal came from...

PIGGY **looks very familiar. You've probably seen a similar looking family of pigs elsewhere, but this isn't a kids cartoon. This is world of danger where everyone is hunting you and you have to do everything you can to not only survive, but to escape.**

To escape, you must work together with other players and find items and keys that can be used to eventually activate the exit. It might be a car that needs fuel, or an exit door that requires power. Some doors have locks on them that can only be opened with the same colour key as the lock. You then need to find a different key for another door. The trick is, you can only hold one item at a time, constantly switching them out.

This is where your teammates come into play. You can each hold important items, giving you more chance to survive. Oh, did we mention that you'll be followed everywhere by a nasty pig holding a weapon?

If you get caught by the hunter you'll be shipped back to the lobby, not before seeing a terrifying screen of you being captured. You'll have plenty of chances to try again, and there are lots of chapters in the story to enjoy.

THERE ARE LOTS OF SKINS TO COLLECT IN THE GAME SHOP. YOU CAN UNLOCK ANY OF THESE USING MONEY COLLECTED DURING A GAME.

SURVIVE THE KILLER!

It's time to *Survive the Killer!*, or **become** them and **chase** other players. Can you **outrun** everyone else and hold out until the exit opens, leading you to freedom?

In this horror game, you get to pretend you're part of a horror film. There's a killer on the loose and if you find yourself as one of the survivors, you must do everything you can to stay alive. This usually means hiding in small spaces and running in the opposite direction when the killer is nearby.

Players can pick up eight items throughout each map which, if you escape alive, will be exchanged for coins to be spent on skins, weapon skins and other cosmetics. It's great fun to try and survive by climbing

onto houses, crawling under fences or hiding inside sheds. But it's terrifying to have the killer chasing you, getting ever closer.

As a change from that nightmare, you could be selected as the killer. Here your job is simple, you must hunt everyone and eliminate them. As one of the killers you'll have different weapons, the challenge comes

from reaching the players constantly running away.

As time ticks on, an exit will open for the players to escape. Reach this in time and you'll win, but a nasty killer could hang around nearby and try to grab players as they think they're about to score a win.

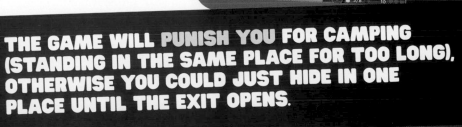

THE GAME WILL PUNISH YOU FOR CAMPING (STANDING IN THE SAME PLACE FOR TOO LONG), OTHERWISE YOU COULD JUST HIDE IN ONE PLACE UNTIL THE EXIT OPENS.

Pre-Run Shop   1,061

Vitamins	100	Lockpick	50
x3 Temporarily boosts speed		x2 May break at any time	
Lighter	50	Flashlight	100
Basic temporary light source		50% Batteries not included	

Thumbsticks to navigate, Ⓐ to press

CONFIRM

DOORS

DOORS has a lot of players. A **LOT** of players. As you might have noticed, these horror games all feature **one thing** - you **need** to escape. That's the same here, except you'll play on much smaller teams while trying to navigate a maze of rooms and **stay clear of monsters**.

From the first room you spawn into, straight off the elevator, you get an idea that *DOORS* is a bit different to other horror games. There's a lot of seeking items and using them to get further, but there are also small puzzles to solve and interesting monsters to avoid.

As you play you will unlock doorknobs, which act like money. You can use this to buy helpful items such as lock picks, a torch or pills that increase your moving speed. These items can be found throughout the rooms you'll explore and are important for reaching later rooms.

Sometimes you'll be stranded in the darkness wishing to find a torch or a

lighter. If you're attacked by a monster, you will want to hunt down a bandage to top up your health. Lockpicks can be helpful if you are unable to find the key to the next room, or if you discover a locked chest.

DOORS will have your nerves jumping like someone on a trampoline. There are times you'll be sat on the edge of your seat, or looking around frantically to find a whispering creature. And moments when your lighter runs out of fuel in long dark corridors may get your hands shaking a little.

Your goal is the final room - Room 100 - which can take a

lot of work. It's not easy, even with three other friends playing alongside you. Think you can master this game? Think again, every time you play the rooms will be different, the monsters appear at new points and the items will have changed around.

Start running for Room 100!

MONSTERS

There is a **scary collection** of monsters to be found in the many rooms of *DOORS*. Each will affect your game in a different way and some may take a long time to even appear for you, but you should **always be ready** to face any of these creatures.

SCREECH - Screech will jump out at you in darkened rooms, robbing you of health. He announces himself by whispering, so if you look at him in time, he won't attack.

RUSH - Rush looks happy, but they're quite nasty. If the lights in your room flicker, get into a wardrobe quickly as Rush will storm through the room destroying everything, including you if they see you.

EYES - Don't look at the eyes! If you even glance at them you'll start losing health.

HALT - This ghostly monster will have you dashing back and forth through a corridor, playing with you. If you don't follow the instructions, you'll lose 60% of your health.

AMBUSH - Ambush is a bit like Rush, except this monster runs through the room several times. If you leave your hiding space too quickly, you'll get hurt or eliminated.

DUPE - Sometimes you'll come across two exit doors. You need to choose the right one by remembering which room you're in. Choose the wrong door and you'll get attacked.

FIGURE - You'll only run into Figure through Door 50 and Door 100. You'll have to solve puzzles while Figure roams around. He can't see you, but his hearing is brilliant. Make sure to sneak!

SEEK - You'll know when Seek has spotted you as they rise from the floor and instantly start chasing you. You must dodge, crouch and dash through a number of rooms while Seek's footsteps thump through your ears. If he catches you, it's game over. Reach the last door in time and Seek gets shut out.

750   1,0

Building, in whichever game, allows players to explore their imagination. Placing blocks, sizing up houses and decorating them with furniture, all give you a little corner of Roblox to call your own. Even tycoons, which require no more than pushing buttons, can feel like a personal space once constructed.

BUILD A BOAT FOR TREASURE

It sounds quite simple, **doesn't it?** To just build a boat that will allow you to **earn treasure**. You just need some wooden planks, right? Not if you've seen the river you need to sail.

There's a long river on which you need to sail, and as you float along you'll slowly earn gold. The only way to do this is to build a boat. You start off in your own little area with a handful of building blocks. Using these you can build a small, rickety raft.

Set sail, and off you go! It might be worth mentioning, the river is full of obstacles big and small. You'll find the obvious - rocks and old broken boats - but you'll also find overly large baseballs and donuts. Hitting any of these will break down your boat and once the last block takes damage, you end up back at the start.

But wait! You've earned some gold which you can spend on new materials for your boat. Slowly but surely, you can put together large, hulking crafts that can survive much more damage allowing you to get further down the river, closer to the treasure.

You can be super serious and craft a boat capable of sailing many nautical miles, or you could just throw everything together and build a ship that looks like a dragon, or a sea monster. As long as it sails, anything goes.

CARNIVAL TYCOON

Your goal is to build the **biggest**, most **fantastic** carnival the world of Roblox has ever seen. The only way to do this is to start **pressing buttons**!

When you see a tycoon, you're probably already thinking you know what's going to happen; you'll be running around stepping on buttons which instantly build parts of your business, or occasionally deposits money you've earnt into your pockets to spend.

And you'd be right - this is a big part of *Carnival Tycoon*, however, what makes this tycoon different, is that you can play all the games in the stalls you build. Want to throw darts and pop balloons? You can

do that. Do you want to throw hoops over targets? This can be done, too.

With each area you buy, you're given a choice of what stall to build. Some are common, so they will come up in the choices more often, others are rare and will attract more customers. Oh, and the customers that attend your carnival are people from your friend list. So, if you see a familiar avatar wandering around, that's because the game is controlling your friends styles.

Sometimes a tycoon will have you standing around doing nothing while you wait for more money to be paid out. Now you can play mini-games while you wait, keeping you busier and more entertained.

33

LAUNDRY SIMULATOR

One of the **best things** about Roblox is how it can make even the most boring activities feel like **fun**. Doing laundry is one of those things. Nobody enjoys laundry, but if you were **earning gold** for each item of clean clothing, you'd enjoy it. That's what happens in this simulator.

Starting off with a small laundry basket and a rusty washing machine, you can collect dirty clothes from a central conveyor belt. **Each item you clean and drop off in the laundry chute rewards you with some cash. This is then spent to buy bigger laundry baskets and better washing machines.**

Those better machines add a multiplier to the cash you earn, plus have bigger capacities for laundry loads. Even more impressive is the silver and gold clothing. If you spot these, grab them fast for a huge boost to your money total. Oh, and you have to be quick as you're surrounded by other players who will swipe it otherwise.

Just to put it in perspective how bonkers this game is, every time the clean laundry chute has 10,000 items deposited, a nuclear bomb drops outside. This stains all incoming clothing for another massive boost in money. Yes, you'll be cleaning clothes during a nuclear explosion.

Definitely a weird game that makes laundry seem cool.

ISLANDS

When you first start playing *Islands*, you may find it a **little familiar**. The game is made up of blocks which can be placed to **create buildings** or **objects**, all while you're adventuring through the world.

Islands **gets its name from the world where you live. It's based on the popular idea of 'skyblocks' where players harvest materials and build objects on small floating islands. If you're unfamiliar with this way of playing a crafting game, there are some helpful missions to guide you along.**

You can start off growing basic crops which can be combined to create food and materials when used on a crafting station will create items of furniture. While you're building, you can use wood or stone to expand your floating

island until it's holding everything you might need.

If you're feeling lonely out on your small island, there is a portal which will transport you to a town full of shops and traders. Here, you can sell the crops you've grown, buy new items you might need and even adopt pets to keep you company.

Once you've reached a point where you have lots of blocks stored away, you can begin to build some huge creations. Let your imagination run wild!

$272

060 MPH 3 00012 MI

CAR DEALERSHIP TYCOON

$5,287   Miles: 32.04

104   5   00032

Tycoon building games often makes **creating** a successful business a lot easier. Usually you're just pressing buttons to craft **particular** sections. With *Car Dealership Tycoon*, it goes a little deeper than that, but keeps everything very **player-friendly**. With an equal split between **building** and **driving**, this is a must-play!

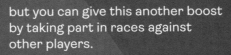

Choosing the right area for your dealership is the first thing to check off your list. You're offered several spaces where your building will be placed, nestling it nicely within the city; and a handy, bright green button will be just outside.

You'll notice this is the only button in this tycoon, and once you press it you'll find a menu with lots of options and prices. In here you can choose to add floors to the building, add new platforms to display cars, and of course, set up a sales desk. All of these additions will earn you extra cash that is used to expand your business.

That's not the only way to make money, this is a driving game too. You can hop into any cars you are displaying and take them for a spin around the map. As you drive, you'll see cash rolling in steadily,

but you can give this another boost by taking part in races against other players.

This creates a loop of earning money, then investing that money into your dealership and buying new cars. The cars themselves are great to play with and range from cheap family cars through to flashy hypercars that break the speed limits.

You can focus on either building or racing, or create a balance of the two. You can really show off your personality, too. Changing the colour schemes of your dealership and naming the business really makes this feel like your place to belong.

Now it's your chance to venture out and make as much money as possible, collect gorgeous cars and become the best salesperson ever.

LOOKING FRESH!

If you play Roblox often, you'll have seen lots of people wandering around during games looking **very fancy**, or **spectacular**. There are so many skins available to really **show off** your creativity, **imagination** and **personality**.

BEST CHARACTERS

STEAMPUNK ROBOT

"Sycamore Cranson was known to build robots from his vast curiosity"

This is a very fancy little robot, built in the Steampunk style which merges the past with the far-flung future. Look at his cute little monocle, and the dials on his shoulders. While he may not be the most spectacular robot, he looks friendly and charming.

250

GANG O'FRIES

"These fries look too delicious for their own good"

There's something funny about items of food turned into people. Or, in this case, lots of people. All bundled together in a cardboard package. Some of them are looking really cranky. If you're a huge fan of fries (and who isn't?!) then you can grab this skin and be the life of the party.

250

All quotes from Robolx's marketplace.

FELIX THE FISHERMAN

"The newest resident of the local lagoon has had some trouble connecting with his neighbours"

Apparently Felix can't make friends easily. It might be because he's only wandering around in his pants, and nothing else. He's pretty scary to look at; with those spiky teeth and big bulging, yellow eyes, meeting him would definitely freak out a lot of people. He looks like he might be friendly though, right? Right?

MR. TOILET

"I was going to tell you a poop joke, but it stinks..."

If it wasn't for the fact that this is clearly a person and a toilet combined, you'd think it was a well stocked potty. There's all the toilet paper you'd need and some plungers just in case. We'll skip using this one when we desperately need to go as it looks like the last person didn't flush. Or, is the poop supposed to be hair? Ewwww.

ROBLOX ZOMBIE

"Clearly he's the brains of this outfit"

Sometimes you want to be the bad guy. Other times, you just want to scare the pants off your friends. This zombie skin combines both! You can shamble or chase after your buddies across the servers looking for brains to munch. This zombie looks like they've seen better days as they've lost a leg! Never mind though, they're also 'armless'... haha.

LUCKY GATITO

"One fond, fine, friendly, furry, feline!"

Lucky cats are statues found in Japan, that wave their paws up and down. If they wave their right hands, they are welcoming money and good fortune. They often feature bells around their necks too, so it looks like this cutie skin will keep you company while hopefully offering luck in finding wealth and good health. Look at her big, pointy ears and lovely collar. She's a special kitty.

Sometimes you don't want an **entire outfit** or **skin** to show off your personality. By combining clothing and accessories you can personalise your avatar in **thousands** of ways. This gives you the chance to dress up however you like - as a **person**, or even a **magical creature**.

BEST ACCESSORIES

DARKENED WENDIGO ANTLERS

Why not give yourself some antlers and appear as a fantastical creature who stumbled from the forest?

60

GIANT DARK ANGEL WINGS

300

Equipping a pair of wings will give you that angelic, or demonic look. A supreme being stepping into the world of Roblox.

EMERALD KNIGHT OF THE SEVENTH SANCTUM ORACLE

Phew, what a mouthful! It's a good job this mask makes you look like a super wizard, with long pointy horns and neon green glasses built in.

100

WHITE CALICO CAT TAIL

100

Some accessories can let you fulfil a wish to be part of the animal kingdom. With this kitty tail, you can look super cute.

HUGGY DINO SUIT

100

We've all seen those inflatable dinosaur suits on YouTube, now it's your chance to wear one in Roblox and make everyone around you giggle.

MIDNIGHT MOTORCYCLE

750

Sometimes you just need to arrive at the venue in style. This black, chrome and neon motorbike looks incredible day or night. So, pull up and impress your friends.

FLOPPA SHOULDER PET

Having a cute and cuddly friend sit on your shoulder can instantly transform an outfit from boring to adorable. This little cutie looks like the best friend you can have.

99

BLACK TV HEAD

100

Have you always wanted to be on TV? This is your chance, but not in the way you're thinking. Instead of being on TV, you're the actual TV.

FISHTANK

You don't really look like a diver with this Fishtank surrounding your avatar. You'll feel more like a fish while floating in the water. Just don't tap on the glass!

100

MILK DRINK HAT

Milk is so good for you. It makes your bones nice and strong. So, it's good to get your daily portion of calcium. What better way to do this than with a hat that keeps you constantly drinking?

70

SANDWICH COSTUME

100

Can we have a cheese and salad sandwich, on Italian bread, please? This is not what we had in mind when we requested that tasty sandwich.

USAGI MASK

25

If you want a great mask based on Japanese folktales, you have to grab this one. It's both traditional, while also being kawaii.

RAINBOW GAMER MECH ARMS SUIT V2

These mech arms not only make you look cool, but they make you look much tougher. Can you imagine the battles you could win with these crushing, mechanical arms?

195

BLACK MILITARY MECHA WAIST GUNS

65

Obviously, these guns don't actually shoot, but they look very cool. Imagine jumping into a shooting game and looking this awesome and dangerous.

GREYSCALE BABY CHICK PET HAT

OMG! So cute! This tiny baby chick will happily chill out on your head, as if your hair was a comfy nest.

89

CORGI BACKPACK

It's 'take your pet to work day' so what better way to keep your pet close, than to snuggle them into your backpack. There's no denying that corgis are adorable, but this little doggo will melt everyone's hearts.

100

COMPETITION TIME! C

DO YOU HAVE

WIN!

One of the coolest things about Roblox is that you can get really creative with how your avatar looks, summing up you and your personality in one image. The avatar store is filled with millions of items for you to combine and show off your style.

Simply send us a screenshot of your avatar, and the GamesWarrior team will pick their 20 favourite avatars to feature in a future GamesWarrior title. So, let's see your craziest, or coolest avatar!

20 WINNERS WILL GET...

their avatar published in a future GamesWarrior title!

PLUS

an advanced copy of the GamesWarrior title with their avatar inside.

HOW TO ENTER

STEP 1
Take a screenshot of your avatar.

STEP 2
Send your screenshot to competitions@littlebrotherbooks.co.uk by the 31st March 2024.

Use 'Roblox 2024 Edition Competition' as the subject of the email.

Include your name, age, postal address and contact email address.

You must ask your parent or guardian's permission to enter the competition.

THE BEST AVATAR?

0/4

COMPETITION TERMS & CONDITIONS

Roblox is a massively multiplayer game, with millions of players jumping in to play together. What better way to play with others than to play against them? PvP (Player Vs Player) can be found everywhere, across various games, and most of them are an absolute blast.

BIG PAINTBALL!

Can you band together with your team to **secure a win** on the paintball fields? Get out there and equip your favourite weapon, then be ready to **eliminate** as many players as possible.

One hit from a paintball will see you eliminated and back in your base to try again. That may sound unfair, but you'll be back in the game in no time at all.

For each elimination you score you'll get points that can be used to unlock new weapons. Each of these plays very differently; an SMG will spray paintballs at close range; a rifle can hit players far away; an assault rifle hits that middle ground. There are so many weapons we could fill several pages of this book. That's before we even talk about abilities earned, like radars and turrets.

The sound of the paintballs being fired is so satisfying. It's not quite ASMR, but it's close. The little pop-pop-pop they make is delightful. It's a happy sound in an otherwise hectic and chaotic game. Several teams are dropped into a map and told to beat the others by eliminating players by landing paintball shots.

Players can be found jumping all over the place, hiding in corners, dashing towards swarms of enemies, and generally causing mayhem. Paint splatters everywhere, turrets appear and hose people down, sending them back to spawn quickly. *BIG Paintball!* is serving up some great PvP.

The bullets will stop being fired in 14 seconds; jump between them to reach the top

13:05:40   **Missions**

30   Win Accurate Archery

30   Win 3 team min

30   Win Survive the Spheres

30   Kill 3 Purchase VIP words

The adventure will end in 67 seconds; find your way to the hidden treasure

EPIC MINIGAMES

Can you become the **best player** in the lobby, by mastering the mini games quickly? There's **a lot to learn** while playing against a lobby filled with other players.

There are over 120 mini games to play and they come in all shapes and sizes. One moment you'll be jumping on overly large moving cannonballs, continually jumping upwards to reach the safe zone and win. Another game will see players dodging lots of snow from an avalanche. There's some prop hunting available, that has players disguising themselves as objects while others try to find them.

It can take a little while to learn the different games as they are all unique. Some require a bit of parkour, some use your memory. To master them all will take some time!

Each game often features more than one winner, so it's simple to finish many of the games and score yourself some points and coins. Levelling up your avatar here unlocks great items and pets, which are bought with the coins.

It all feels like a gameshow where everyone is expressing themselves in terrific ways, with fancy outfits and accessories. All it's missing is a host to make cheesy jokes and hand out the prizes.

Seekers will be released in 4 seconds; hiders must find a place to hide

FRONT LINES

Front Lines is a **realistic shooter** game that takes inspiration from *Call of Duty*. But if you think it's going to look like a normal Roblox game, you're in for a **huge surprise**.

Go back a page and look at *BIG Paintball!* then look at *Front Lines*. The graphics, as well as the gameplay itself, are completely different. So much so, you'd think you weren't even on Roblox anymore.

Front Lines is mostly a team shooter. It features realistic environments as well as realistic weapons that can be upgraded piece by piece, completely changing how the weapon feels when

playing. Where other PvP games rely on wacky moments and bonkers creativity, this feels more tactical and serious.

And it can be brutal. The precision needed to eliminate people can vary from accurate sniping to lucky grenade throws. If you can master it, there are a lot of hours that can be spent tuning the weapons and levelling up your character.

IF YOU LOVE THIS, THEN CHECK OUT *PHANTOM FORCES*, WHICH IS ONE OF THE ORIGINAL REALISTIC SHOOTERS ON ROBLOX.

JAILBREAK

In the world of *Jailbreak*, you can either play for **good** or **bad**, **police** or escaped **criminal**. You'll probably find one of these much more fun, and that's entirely down to how you like to play.

As a police officer, you'll be responsibe for protecting the city and capturing the escaped prisoners. With a police car, weapon and handcuffs, you can play nice or a little more unfair, as long as you keep the streets clean of criminals.

On the flip side, you can play as a prisoner who starts off behind bars. Once you escape, you have nothing to your name; unlike the police who start out with the right equipment, you have to find your way. This means pulling off heists and robberies so you can buy cars and weapons.

Whichever side you choose, you'll be playing against other players who all want one thing - to be the best cop, or the richest criminal. Both are a challenge; you can team up with friends to rob a jewellery store, which a lone cop won't be able to stop. Or you can all join the force and find those lone criminals to arrest and take back to jail.

The city you have to explore is huge! It's filled with all manner of buildings, as well as farms, fields, stretches of road and large places of interest. When it feels like you've seen it all, you'll drive a little further down a road to find something new to explore. Or rob. Or defend. It's all up to you.

ARSENAL

Race to the top through a **massive** arsenal of weapons! *Arsenal* is one of, if not the, best shooting game on Roblox. This one is **always** **popular** and receives new content quite often, while staying **very** **competitive**. *Arsenal* isn't an overly realistic shooter, but it has enough depth to keep players coming back **constantly**.

Arsenal **spins out from a classic game mode seen before in many shooters over the years – gun game. *Arsenal* sees players drop into a map with a random weapon and the goal is to eliminate the other teams. The catch is, every time you score an elimination your weapon changes.**

This means you might start out with a pistol, land a kill and see your gun switch to a sniper rifle.

With *Arsenal*, it's not limited to just guns, though. A weapon switch might give you a spell book, or a wacky weapon you could never even think of.

As with so many other games in this book, playing equals rewards. In Arsenal you get BattleBux, which can be exchanged for new skins or cases where the reward is completely random. Everything in this game is random!

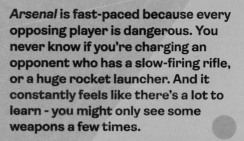

Arsenal is fast-paced because every opposing player is dangerous. You never know if you're charging an opponent who has a slow-firing rifle, or a huge rocket launcher. And it constantly feels like there's a lot to learn - you might only see some weapons a few times.

The maps are pretty big too. There's a lot of variation between each map and you'll quickly find your favourite. The variety in the maps makes *Arsenal* feel a bit more complex as certain maps are better for long-range play, while others make melee weapons more useful. It's all a balancing act as you make your way to the top.

WHILE THE WEAPONS HERE ARE ALWAYS RANDOM, THAT RULE GOES OUT THE WINDOW AS YOU NEAR A POSSIBLE WIN. WHEN PLAYING SOLO, YOU NEED TO SCORE 32 ELIMINATIONS TO WIN THE GAME. WHEN PLAYING FOR THE 31ST KILL, YOU'RE ALWAYS GIVEN A GOLDEN GUN; AND ON KILL 32 YOU GET A GOLDEN KNIFE. KILLS WITH THESE GOLDEN WEAPONS TURNS THE OPPOSING PLAYER INTO A GOLDEN STATUE AND YOU WIN THE GAME.

Standard

Each elimination or assist will give you a new weapon. Reach the Golden Knife for a final elimination to win!

Going fast is exciting. Whether that's behind the wheel of a supercar, or sprinting along with superhuman speed. Many Roblox games give you the skills or machinery needed to break the speed limits. How fast will you go? Can you break the sound barrier, or wow your slow-poke friends?

SHOCKWAVE RACING

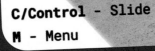

C/Control - Slide

M - Menu

Shockwave Racing is a **parkour-speedrunning** game where each level is randomly generated every time you play. No course will **ever** be the same!

As soon as you start to play *Shockwave Racing*, you'll notice the speed. This is a super fast game where stopping should be avoided at all times. If you want to be competitive and beat the other players, you need to finish the course as many times as possible within the time limit.

You'll have to act fast as you move here, jumping by instinct, skimming the platforms before you leap again towards another. At the same time you'll be dodging lasers which rotate, move side-to-side or appear from nowhere. The whole time you're constantly watching out for what obstacle comes next because if you fall, or are hit by a laser, you'll be sent back to the start.

It feels so good to nail a course and make every jump, but it's even better when you can do it several times in the time limit and score a bunch of coins to spend in the shop.

DRIVING SIMULATOR

There are **so many** driving games on Roblox; *Driving Simulator* combines racing, exploring, great graphics and **brilliant car handling**.

The first car you get in Driving Simulator is a small, rather slow car. It's nothing flash, more of a family car than a racer. It's fine for cruising around the city seeing the sights, which is a steady way to make money. As your car is whizzing through the streets, your bank balance will grow and you can invest in a better car.

As soon as you've chosen a new car - a faster car - the world around you becomes a blur and you'll be ready to jump into some races. As you drive around you'll notice large circles on the road which, when driven through, will enter you into a race. Races can be tricky as there are lots of players with speedy supercars, but if you win you can bag a lot of cash.

Perhaps the best thing about *Driving Simulator* is collecting the cars. There's so much variety here; you can find hypercars that costs millions, bizarre vehicles that would look out of place in real life, all the way down to police cars. And they're all yours to buy, keep and race all over the city.

SPEED RUN 4

If you want a speedy game, you can't go wrong here, **it's in the name!** *Speed Run 4* is another parkour game where you'll need to **jump** across a variety of platforms to reach the end.

It is very easy to fall off these platforms. They can be tiny. Plus, your avatar is running incredibly fast. It's okay though, if you fall, you'll head back to the start with the extra knowledge of the platforms and the angles you'll need to jump.

So, you might be thinking, 'why should I play this?' The answer is, the environments. There's so much wonderful imaginativeness to see. Racecourses look like they're from outer space, or torn from the pages of a comicbook.

Don't get ahead of yourself though, *Speed Run 4* can be really difficult, especially in the later levels. This is a great game to play with friends so you can challenge each other and see who gets the furthest, or who can reach a certain level the fastest.

Get running!

★ 2 ■ 16
00:12.68

SKIP LEVEL ➡

You got 2 gems for beating Level 5!
■ 2 ■ 26
00:04.70

Store
Items
Dimension

SKIP LEVEL ➡

19

🐦 📊

🛒 **Store**

📦 **Items**

◎ **Dimension**

SKIP LEVEL ➡

FLY RACE!

Fly Race! is a great game if you like numbers, and seeing those **numbers stack up**. Plus, you'll be soaring through the air the **whole** time, too.

In _Fly Race!_ the idea is simple, jump the furthest and reach for the highest scores. You do this by running up a ramp and launching into the distance. At first, your jumps will be tiny; they will barely score any money. Collecting rocket icons can boost your jump power and the further away you land, the more cash you'll be rewarded with.

That money is very important, as it will fuel your jumps by purchasing pets. These pets act

like little rockets strapped to your body. Your jumps will start stretching out and you'll spend more time in the air. The better the pets, or the rarer they are, the further you jump

It's all about gaining power, getting faster, and scoring big. After a while, you'll be flying, screaming along the course with no slowing down, adding up countless laps. Once you land, that money total will be going crazy, and the numbers growing and growing.

Despite the speed, this game is actually very relaxing as it takes very little control; you set everything up and just keep jumping.

DOWNFORCE STUNT DRIVING

We're back to cars, but we're not just **speeding** through the city streets this time. Hold onto your butt, as we're going to make these cars do things they **weren't designed for!**

The world of *Downforce* looks just like a regular city, however down by the coast you'll notice there are ramps, loops and walls, all interconnected. Your goal is to pull off some sick stunts in various cars, starting with a small, slower vehicle.

It's quite easy to get a stunt going - all you need to do is drive as fast as possible at the ramp and you car will immediately stick to the track. There's a handy boost button if your car begins to slow, and this will force you along any surface.

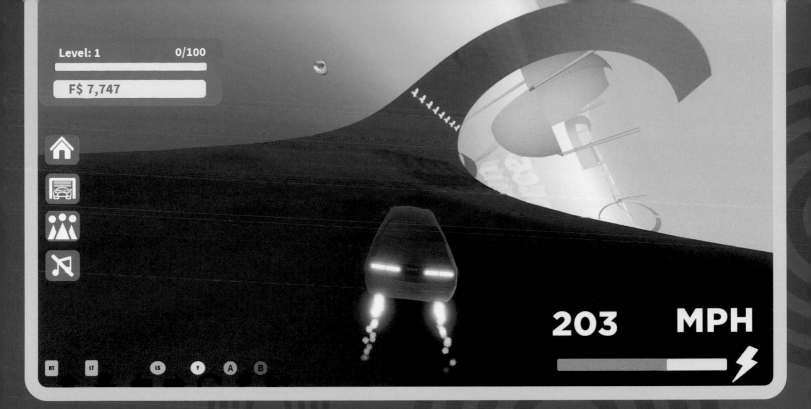

It feels thrilling to be driving upside down in a loop, or stuck to a wall while your boost is burning. There are players zipping everywhere around you, battling for space on the obstacles. Thankfully, the cars all handle really well, so moving through tight corners will never be an issue.

A big highlight are the huge ramps that are scattered around the city. Grab some friends and all make your way to the top, then get ready to fly. Making these jumps on your own, you'll feel like a superhero, but with your buddies, the whole crew looks iconic as you exit the ramp side-by-side.

Every stunt you manage to pull off will reward you with cash, which can be spent on new cars. There is no need for a super fast car to hit the stunts, but faster cars will make for longer jumps that look amazing.

Choose your car, fasten your seat belt and start speeding through the streets, or flying into the sky.

Roblox can be a fun way to learn - there are plenty of games that try to teach you things like maths, history, geography and much more. Did you know that during the Covid pandemic teachers across the world picked up Roblox to continue teaching kids who couldn't go to school?

MATH OBBY

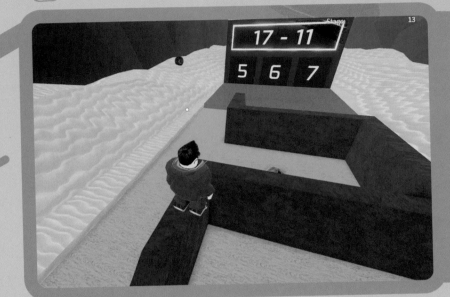

MATH OBBY

A nice, simple way to learn the basics of maths is to attempt this obby. The game is broken down into math topics - addition, subtraction, etc. Players are presented with a maths problem and several potential answers. You must travel across the obby to the correct answer.

If you get it wrong, don't worry, you can try again. *Math Obby* is such a fun and creative way to work on those tricky maths equations.

FARMING AND FRIENDS

FARMING AND FRIENDS

Farming makes the world go round. Without farmers working hard on their fields, millions of people would go hungry. *Farming and Friends* lets you learn by doing. It's up to you to learn how to plow fields, plant seeds and harvest crops.

There are lots of different seeds, as well as machinery to master. The longer you play, and the more you achieve, you'll start to unlock more and more options. Playing games like this gives you a chance to see how certain jobs work.

ROBLOX TITANIC

ROBLOX TITANIC

You've probably already heard of the ship, *Titanic*. It was a huge luxury liner that, on its first voyage, struck an iceberg and tragically sank. Many of the passengers on that fateful journey lost their lives in the freezing sea.

Roblox Titanic gives you an opportunity to be one of those passengers and learn exactly what happened on board after the ship hit the iceberg. You can explore the bedroom cabins, the dining hall, grand staircase and the engine operating rooms. Of course, this tragedy cannot be avoided, and you will eventually have to escape on a lifeboat as you watch the beautiful ship sink.

EXPEDITION ANTARTICA

EXPEDITION ANTARTICA

The first person to ever reach the South Pole did so in 1912. It's hard to imagine people travelling to the Earth's southern pole. The freezing climate can break even the toughest people. You can learn a lot about how these expeditions took place by trying this game.

Of course, a real expedition doesn't feature an obby every few minutes, but it would be a little dull to just walk through bright, white spaces. This game lets you take a peek at the equipment needed to take on such a journey. At least you can learn while at home, in the warm.

If you're new to Roblox it's tough to know which games to start with. Some games have been around for years and can feel overwhelming, while others may not suit your taste in games. It's nice to know where to begin, and to get a feel for the various experiences. Here are some great games to get you started.

CAR CRUSHERS 2

If you want to take a moment out of life to **destroy things**, causing **complete mayhem**, then *Car Crushers 2* might be the perfect game for you.

The game is simple, all you need to do is drive vehicles into different traps and watch them be completely smashed to pieces. To list all the different ways of doing this would take hours, but for a little taste of what's ahead, you can:

- Drop your car into a pit of spinning blades.
- Create a wall of lasers which will chop up your car.
- Drive the vehicle down a flight of stairs.

- Chop a car into pieces using huge butcher knives.
- Speed a high-power car into a solid brick wall.

With each of these, and many others, the vehicles break up into a beautiful mess of parts and each destruction is accompanied by a satisfying crunch. What's great is that you do this over and over again, earning money and parts to buy new vehicles and unlock new traps. It's a simple, easy game to introduce you to the chaos of Roblox.

ULTIMATE EASY OBBY

'Obby' is short for 'Obstacle'. Obstacle courses are **very popular** on Roblox, with thousands of Obbys available to play. They all scale in difficulty, but you're going to want a **nice easy start** before you tackle the harder courses.

In *Ultimate Easy Obby* you'll be slowly introduced to the different obstacles; they start with basic movement, like running and jumping, before challenging you to make bigger leaps over dangerous objects.

After a while, you'll get used to the movement and be tasked with a really tricky parkour, like jumping into the air and changing direction as you leap. But don't worry, you have to move on from simple parkour sooner or later and this will have built up your confidence.

Once you've explored everything in this Obby, which is a great starting point, you can search for 'Obby' on Roblox and start to experience some brilliant creations. There are hundreds of themes, from different colours, to K-Pop, to ultra-difficult. Enjoy the new challenges!

CITY RUSH TYCOON

Tycoon games are **all about money**. Players need to use a steady flow of cash to build businesses, houses, schools, carnivals, and in this example, **cities**.

Tycoons are one of the easiest games to learn on Roblox. Many of them, which you'll see here, requires nothing more than walking across buttons. You'll start small, pressing a button to receive cash, then more buttons to start off construction.

Each button you then see has a larger money total needed to press it. This

creates or builds larger objects or buildings. In *City Rush Tycoon* each button, which is only pressed once, will construct buildings, skyscrapers, beaches, fast food restaurants and lines of beautiful trees.

With each piece of the city built, more money will flow into your bank, then more buildings will spring up. This

repeats until you have a wonderful city to roam through. *City Rush Tycoon* asks a bit more of you compared to other tycoons, though. Occasionally your city residents will be unhappy because of fires, robberies, or electrical problems in buildings, you must fix these issues or lose money.

Now you've learned the basics of tycoons, it's worth looking for some other games that meet your interests. Maybe you want to create a theme park, or a school. Time to build!

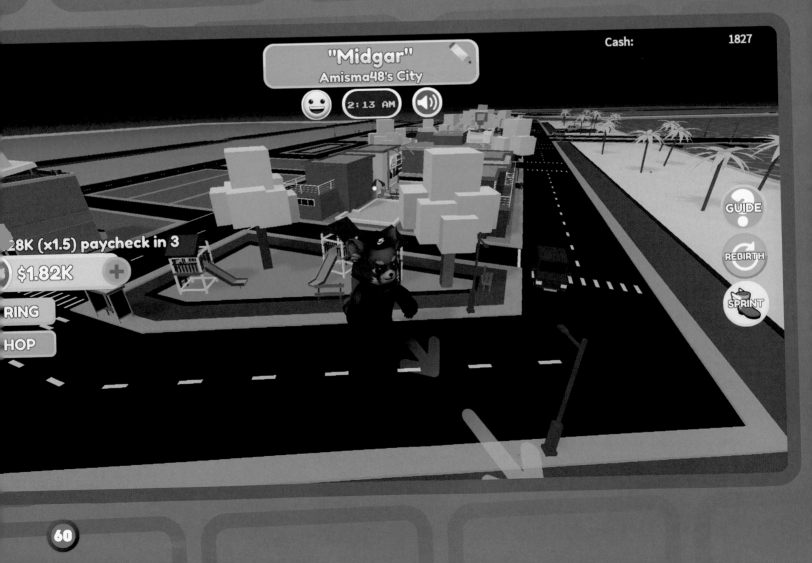

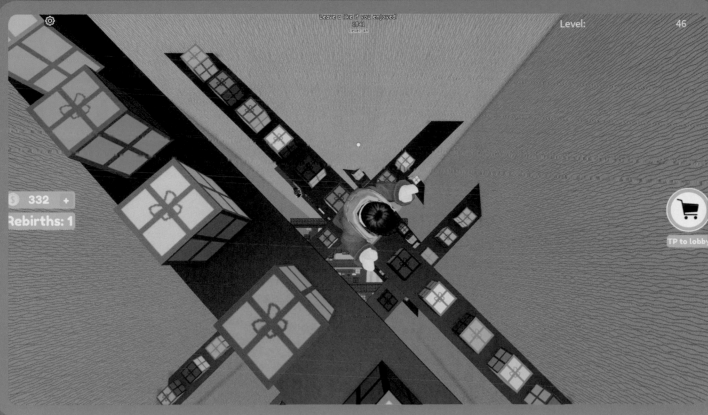

THE DROPPER

Droppers originated in Minecraft and have begun appearing in many other games. You'll need some **quick reflexes** in this dropper game, but every level will make you feel like a **champion**.

Droppers are perhaps the simplest games around. Players will jump into a pit in the ground and must dodge all the obstacles on the way down to the exit. If you touch any of the items, your avatar will explode. If you touch a wall, your avatar explodes. Basically, touch anything except the the exit and you'll explode.

The Dropper has a huge variety of courses to drop through. There are tacos, hoops, criss-crossed lasers; you name it and there's probably a dropper level here.

Think of these like the obbys, but gravity affects every movement you make. Beating tricky levels will have you feeling great, especially if it's one you've been stuck on for some time. Jump in and see how far you can get without dying.

GARTEN
OF BANBAN

Banban's kindergarten is a **very spooky** place to be, but it's a **great** horror game to explore before you jump into some others.

When you first spawn into the kindergarten (which is a school for young children) you'll find the lights dimmed and a strange silence throughout the rooms. The first thing you need to do is explore. You'll quickly find a keycard that opens up a door to a storage room where you'll find a remote-control **drone. This drone becomes your main tool for the game.**

From this point on, you need to make your way through the school finding more keycards, pressing buttons and, above all, avoiding really creepy enemies.

This game can be played alone, or with up to three friends. The fear eases if playing with friends, but those jump scares might still chill your bones. You'll always be watching out the corner of your eye incase Banban, or one of his friends, is peeking around a corner.

Horror games are among the most popular on Roblox - there are so many to try. *Garten of Banban* is a perfect introduction because you can take everything slowly and solve the puzzles without a player or bot hunting you down.

The puzzles themselves are very clever and it's helpful to learn how these games work. Usually, there's an item to find which unlocks a door, where you'll find another item or key to move through a different area. Once you've learned this, you'll easily master the mechanics of horror games.

THE MONSTERS

YOU PLAY AS A PARENT WHOSE CHILD HAS GONE MISSING INSIDE THE KINDERGARTEN AFTER THE MONSTER MASCOTS WENT CRAZY AND THE SCHOOL CLOSED ITS DOORS.

- **Banban** – is a tall, red monster with two party hats perched on his oval head. While he doesn't have teeth, he has a scary long tongue.
- **NabNab** – A tall, skinny, purple monster with three eyes.
- **Slow Seline** - A giant yellow snail who creeps slowly.
- **Jumbo Josh** - A large green monster who is very excited about kids eating fruit and veg.

BEST GAMES OF 2023

With over **40 million** games across Roblox it would be impossible to play them all. Thankfully, you can easily discover what are the **most popular** games, with millions of players logging in to enjoy them. Here are the **top ten** games of 2023.

BLOX FRUITS

An adventure game based on popular anime is a sure fire way to get hundreds of thousands of players leaping in. This action game gives you a chance to battle tough enemies and even harder bosses, while sailing across the world. With lots of powers to be found through Fruits that spawn, you can play exactly how you want.

BROOKHAVEN RP

Role-play games are here to stay. What better way to live out a different life online? In *Brookhaven*, you can be anyone you want to be - a racing driver, a model, a parent or a fashion icon. You could live your normal life in the city, or live out your dreams. Grab your friends and set up a community where you can shop, live and explore together.

ADOPT ME!

Everyone has heard of *Adopt Me!* and with good reason. *Adopt Me!* is the best game of all-time on Roblox. With hundreds of pets to adopt and call your own, there's so much to do. New pets come out regularly, there are places to explore with your friends and you can even trade duplicate pets with other players. Or, if you'd rather not trade, upgrade them to neon pets instead.

MURDER MYSTERY 2

In *Murder Mystery 2* you have a chance to solve crimes and catch a killer on the loose. Whether you play with friends or strangers, you can take on various roles to live out a traditional murder mystery. Of course, if you want to play on the dark side, you can become the killer instead and eliminate all the innocents before the sheriff hunts you down.

PET SIMULATOR X!

If you want to become the richest person on a server, then *Pet Simulator X!* might be the best way to do it. You can go from small change to billions of gold by using squads of pets to harvest piles of materials. The pets are key - with hundreds of different pets you can start a great collection, but that's not all... you can fuse your pets together, or transform them into golden versions for that extra swag.

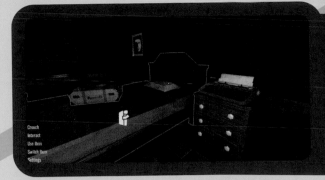

DOORS

Horror games are the biggest thing in Roblox. You can't browse far without finding a horror game, and *DOORS* is one of the best, and easily the most popular. All you have to do is get to door 100, sounds simple, right? But you have to avoid lots of monsters and obstacles; hunt down keys to open doors; collect coins to buy helpful items; and solve puzzles to keep moving forward.

STRONGMAN SIMULATOR

So many games want you to be the richest or most popular, but *Strongman Simulator* asks you to become the strongest. By lifting weights and pushing the limit of a workout, you can grow those muscles and become super strong. It's like being a superhero, but without the cape. Jump in, bulk up and see if you can rule the server!

BEDWARS

PvP is a big part of Roblox, and the most popular multiplayer game has to be *BedWars*. Inspired by popular *Minecraft* games, *BedWars* is a chaotic action game where you must protect a bed in your base. You can defend with blocks, building around the bed; or you can go on the offensive and attack the opposing players and their beds.

WORK AT A PIZZA PLACE

One of the longest running games on Roblox is still one of the most popular. Working at a pizza place might sound boring but there's so much to do! You can work in several roles at the pizza restaurant earning money to develop and decorate your home. Or perhaps you just want to be the best pizza deliverer you can be.

BACKROOMS

Another horror game, though this time based on a YouTube short film. The *Backrooms* are a spooky place to be. You never know what's around the next corner, could it be a friendly player, or a gruesome monster waiting to eliminate you? All you need to do is survive, but to do so, you'll need to be fast, and brave.

Games are a great way to escape into another world, or another life. Perhaps you've always wanted to catch ghosts, or train to be the toughest fighter in the world. Roblox allows anyone to explore their imagination and pretend to be someone else, even for just a short time.

GHOST SIMULATOR

Do you want to **hunt down ghosts** and spooky **monsters**? You can battle through different worlds, finding all kinds of scary beasts, before eliminating them for their value.

After picking up the first few quests in *Ghost Simulator*, you'll be in a rhythm. Players can head out into the world and suck ghosts into their backpacks, ready to be sold to the crazy scientists. Using money from busting ghosts, you can upgrade your ghost fighting equipment, or unlock larger backpacks. There are even pets to unlock who help in capturing ghosties.

But there's more to this than just finding and capturing spirits. There are races to be played against other players and there are more quests which take you through a great story about your place in this haunted world.

Perhaps the most fun are the world bosses who spawn in and require people from all across the server to take them down. These huge monsters can only be beaten by groups of players, so you can take part even if you're new to the game. Just get out there and do your best!

RESTAURANT TYCOON 2

Maybe you want to be a chef. This is something easily achieved on Roblox. In *Restaurant Tycoon 2* players start off with a **tiny restaurant** with only a couple of tables and begin to **build an empire**.

When the first customers arrive, you'll sit them at their table, take their order, then travel into the kitchen to cook up the food they asked for. Of course, being on your own means you'll have to deliver the food to the table. When they leave, you can collect the dirty dishes, pick up the money for the meal and be happy with another satisfied customer.

As your bank balance grows, it's time to expand. Not just the restaurant - by adding more tables and chairs - but by adding new food to the menu, hiring staff to help cook or clean. You can even focus on particular food from around the world; if you want to serve only Japanese food, that is entirely possible.

At some point your business will outgrow the building and you'll be able to go even further, by extending the building and adding more luxurious items. Now you're on your way to becoming the best restaurant owner in the universe.

MINING
SIMULATOR 2

Mining is a **great job** to have. Miners can explore caves that spread out into the Earth, looking for **precious gems**, **metals** and **fossils**. Be careful though, with so many miners around, the ground might collapse on top of you.

Mining at the start of your career is slow going. Your tools are cheap and weak, your backpack is tiny and you'll have to keep travelling to the surface to empty it, earning gold coins. Other miners, those who have been underground for a lot longer, will be speedily digging up the dirt in long columns.

It's hard work, but you'll keep on going. Keep on digging. Once your pockets feel a little fatter from all the gold coins, you can seek out a better pickaxe or shovel. You can choose a larger backpack which will hold a lot more materials, meaning fewer trips to the surface to sell the valuable ore.

Next door to the tool shop is a collection of pet eggs. Hatching these will reward you with pets of all different rarities. These little critters help you dig faster, meaning you can make money quickly. You can stick with the rarest or begin to create a little collection. Either way, keep on digging!

WINDS OF FORTUNE

Perhaps the one job everyone wants at some point – if you can call it a job – is to be a **pirate**. Imagine **sailing the seas**, fighting **monsters** and other pirates on your journey to dig up **treasure**. Arrr, that's the life!

And that's exactly what happens in *Winds of Fortune.* **As a pirate captain, players will travel the world looking for precious maps that lead to treasure buried in the sands of time. There are plenty of islands out there, some hold riches beyond your imagination, while others are home to horrible monsters.**

This is the life of a pirate; running missions to scrape together coins and gems which will make you rich. The sailing is peaceful, until the bad guys show up; exploring is lovely, until skeletons climb up from underground and you have to defend yourself.

Winds of Fortune is one of those games where you think you'll only play for a while and suddenly you've been playing for weeks, searching out rare treasure or seeing the many corners of the world. Pull in some buddies and form yourself a pirate crew, yo-ho!

ANIME FRUIT SIMULATOR

So many Roblox games have a similar goal - to become the **richest**, or the **best**, or the **strongest**. With *Anime Fruit Simulator*, you're tasked with becoming the **best pirate** there ever was, or will be. You do this through battles, fighting your way up from the smaller grunt enemies, all the way up to **dangerous** bosses. Along the way, you'll gain wonderful powers given to you by certain fruits.

If all this sounds familiar, that's because this game is inspired by one of the most popular anime shows of all-time, *One Piece*. An anime where characters gained superhero style powers by eating rare fruits.

Anime Fruit Simulator also plays a lot like *Pet Simulator X!* by having you fight and break down enemies who reward you with gold and gems. Strangely, the bad guys never fight back, instead they stand still and take every hit you can throw because they have SO MUCH HEALTH.

Collecting weapons will make your avatar hit harder, as will the pets you can hatch from eggs. The greatest powers come from the fruits you can find throughout the battle areas, or win from a machine in the home base.

Each fruit offers different powers; some can attack a whole area, hitting every enemy around; others pack a huge punch for devastating damage. Whichever you choose, these powers

can tip a battle in your favour. But it doesn't end there.

Using the gems you win in fights, you can combine fruits to create brand new powers that fit how you want to play. You can experiment and find out what works. All you need are a few copies of the fruits.

As players progress through the different areas - unlocking them with gold coins - it becomes harder to

defeat each boss. They take a bit longer because their health pools grow. This is where clever combinations of fruit powers and weapons come into play.

The whole time you're moving forward, sailing to different ports to find more fights, you're steadily working away at becoming the best pirate to ever sail the seas. Journey out, be the best, fight hard, and above all, have fun!

Sometimes being challenged is a must-have aspect for some players. They enjoy a high level of difficulty, even if it might occasionally become frustrating. It's incredibly satisfying to close a game knowing that it challenged your skills, but you beat it. Roblox is host to a lot of tricky games that will have you either scratching your head or sweating.

OBBY BUT YOU'RE A POTATO

Yes, you definitely read that right. It's an obby - a very **normal** obby - but you don't control your avatar, you have to **control a potato!**

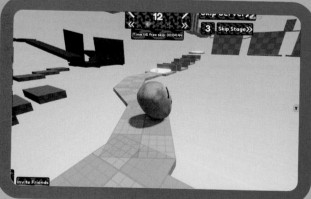

Why is that hard? Well, imagine a potato, they're never perfectly round are they? They're often lumpy and bumpy, with bits that stick out. That would never roll smoothly, and that is the point. How do you make a jump if you aren't sure which way you'll leap or land?

Every jump, movement and landing in this crazy obby is hard to predict. Sometimes the potato will play nicely and roll in a straight line. Other times, it'll wobble all over the place making any jump ten times tougher. You'll have to rely on your usual obby skills, but also adapt them.

One stage will require players to balance along a thin platform, while wobbling, but the next could ask players to jump around walls and land on tiny ledges hanging in open space. There will be plenty of instances when you ask yourself why your even playing this obby, which will have you switching quickly from angry to overjoyed. Keep practicing!

PHANTOM FORCES

Another realistic style shooter here, but one that requires a great deal of **skill** if you want to **survive** and **thrive**. This team game plays like some of the most famous **shooters** from the past few years, completely transforming Roblox.

If you're a skilled shooter player, the gameplay here likely won't trouble you too much. It's a simple recipe, guns + interesting maps = a great action game. What makes this one so tricky is the balance of weapon parts, as you can change out different components on every weapon.

Like so many shooting games on Roblox, these games are becoming more personal than ever. For years, people have come to love certain weapons in games, due to how they feel when playing. Now, this can be further personalised by changing grips, barrels, stocks or ammo on these guns.

Getting that balance is fun, but it means you'll be playing against other players who might have hit a higher level and unlocked better weapons or weapon parts. Getting over that first hurdle is the hardest part - as a brand new player you'll find you get eliminated a lot. As with everything else, practice makes perfect, but having a good team also helps.

If you can play any of these shooter games with friends, you'll have more chance to succeed because you can work together to move around the enemy players and try new tactics.

OPEN MAP

Already owned
You already have Quest Marker

Markers:

OPEN MAP

FIND THE MARKERS

Rather than always relying on **skill**, some games force you to rely on your **brain**. *Find the Markers* is a large game world in which marker pens are **hiding**. Players need to track them all down using clues, **solving** puzzles or **exploring**.

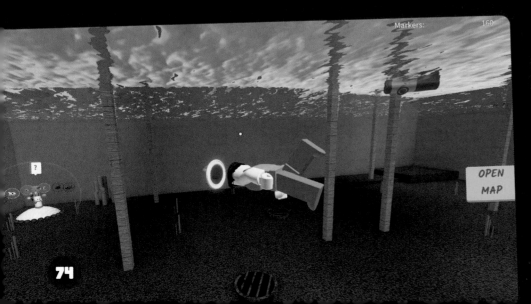

Markers: 160

OPEN MAP

Finding the first few markers is easy. You'll see them hanging around the central area, or stood on hillsides. Touching each marker unlocks them in the catalogue,

where you can see your collection. Each marker has a little clue to find them, but they aren't easy. In fact, the markers are ranked from easy to expert.

The expert markers require a great deal of puzzling - flicking switches in the correct pattern, or finding secret areas which lead to difficult obby challenges. You'll seriously be here for hours, searching high and low, examining every corner of the map.

Then, suddenly, you'll stumble across a portal that transports you to a different world, where even more markers are hiding. You can wander around by yourself, or team up with your friends to puzzle out each marker.

Seeing the collection grow is so satisfying, especially when you begin to find the expert markers.

[PDW-R] Fresh Meat
[PDW-R] Reanimated

Round   Zombies
010 / 0115

RPG-7   KA-BAR

ZOMBIE UPRISING

Zombies are a **problem** in this Roblox world. They are **everywhere**, swarming all areas to breaking point. It's up to you to build barricades, set traps and equip yourself with the **best weapons** to hold back the zombie outbreak.

It doesn't matter how good you are at action games, a zombie is going to get you. You can have the best weapons, set the right traps for your area, and eventually you'll find yourself running backwards, spraying ammo towards the horde of zombies chasing you down.

This is mostly because it's not just zombies coming for you. There are

demons, monstrous skeletons and variants of zombies that will keep moving forward until they are crunching on your bones. Thankfully, you aren't alone. You are grouped with a bunch of players who can not only help you attack these waves of undead, but also revive you if you're caught.

There are stacks of weapons and items you can use to attack or

defend. These cost points which you will collect with each zombie you kill, with a bonus coming at the end of the waves. Remember, they can't eat your brains if you're using them to get away.

75

TOWER OF HELL

In earlier pages we showed you the **easiest obby** on Roblox, but now it's time to go in the opposite direction. *Tower of Hell* is the **hardest** obby you'll encounter for a few reasons, but this doesn't stop it being one of the **most enjoyable** games out there.

Tower of Hell requires all of your obby skills. You'll recognise so many of the obstacles - damaging areas, long jumps, climbing walls and much more. The difficulty here doesn't come from the obstacles on their own, but how they are constructed.

This hellfire obby is created completely randomly every few minutes. You only have a short time to tackle the tower and make it as high as possible before everything resets. Because of the random construction, you'll never play the same tower more than once. This means you can't keep practicing a section until you finally get it.

Not only that, but you're against the clock. You can't keep stopping to judge your jumps, or work out how to move through a section because you'll fall behind. They key is to play by instinct, jump when it feels right, and fly by the seat of your pants.

Making it even more challenging is the fact that you're playing alongside other people. While this can help sometimes, as you'll see how they tackle a section, it can also hold you back when so many players are surrounding you. But, if you're really cheeky you can dash past them and get in their way instead.

The best games that offer up difficulty strike a fine balance between being tough and being fair. *Tower of Hell* does this really well. Yes, it's a tricky game, but really, everything is just a hop, skip and a jump away from you.

STAYING SAFE WHILE HAVING FUN

FOR PLAYERS

PICKING A USERNAME
NEVER choose a username that has your personal information, such as your real name or birthday.

STAY SECRET
Don't ever give out your real name, address, phone number, or the school you go to. Roblox will never need this info, and neither will anyone else. Roblox has chat software that will automatically try to filter out real-life names for a reason.

STAY IN-GAME
Scammers may ask you to trade money or items outside of the game. That's a good way to lose things. The trading menu in Roblox is designed to protect you, so stick to that and never give anything to people outside the game, no matter how trustworthy they may appear.

DON'T BE AFRAID TO REPORT
Players can easily mute and report inappropriate or abusive chat message, or disturbing content. Just use the Report Abuse system that's located on every single menu and Roblox will be notified and take action as soon as possible.

TELL YOUR PARENTS
Be brave. If someone is bothering you or you saw something you didn't like, tell a parent or guardian. Don't be afraid to say if someone is being inappropriate on Roblox. This game is for everyone and no one should be made to feel unsafe!

"I HEARD ABOUT A ROBUX GENERATOR!"
There are no such things as Robux Generators – they're made up by scammers to steal money and accounts from players. Don't fall for it. Never trust any websites that aren't official. All official websites end with '.roblox.com'.

FOR PARENTS

BE INVOLVED
The best thing parents can do to make sure their children stay safe playing Roblox is to simply talk to them about the dangers. Make an account for yourself as you make one for your child. You'll even be able to add them as your child on Roblox, allowing you to ensure the social aspects of the game aren't getting in the way of them having fun.

SAFETY FEATURES
You can sign into your child's account and choose the level of privacy that they have. Make sure you choose the correct date of birth for your child as it sets the default security settings depending on how old they are. You can further modify the settings so that no one can contact your child, or that everyone can. Older players have more options.

MESSAGES AND CHAT
You can easily view your child's private message and chat histories from the main screen. You can also see your child's online friends, the games they've made, and anything they've purchased. If anything looks off, you can then take action.

PROTECTING YOUNGER CHILDREN
While Roblox is tamer than most games, some games feature violence or scary situations. You can go to the Account Restrictions section of your child's account to restrict them from playing anything too intense for their age group.

"MY KID IS BEING BULLIED"
If someone is bothering your child, you should report and block them. By clicking on a username you can easily block a user and prevent them from ever contacting your child. By reporting abuse you can make sure that Roblox is aware of the situation.

FOR MANY MORE RESOURCES WE RECOMMEND GOING TO ROBLOX'S OFFICIAL PARENT'S GUIDE AT: WWW.CORP.ROBLOX.COM/PARENTS THERE YOU'LL FIND TUTORIALS FOR NAVIGATING THE PLATFORM, AS WELL AS TIPS FOR ONLINE SAFETY.